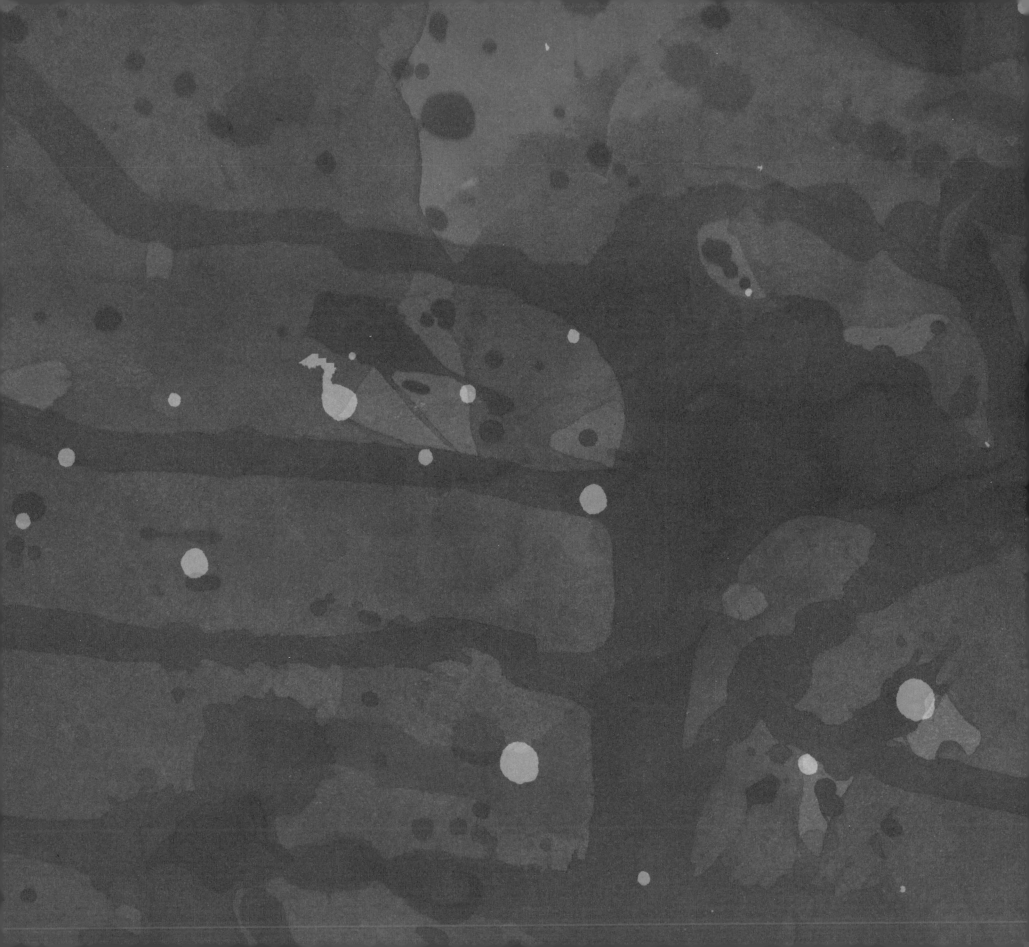

~THIS~
DROP OF
WATER

Franklin Watts

First published in Great Britain in 2018 by The Watts Publishing Group

Credits

Editor: Julia Bird

Designer: Jeni Child

HB ISBN 978 1 4451 6365 9

PB ISBN 978 1 4451 6364 2

Printed in China

FSC
www.fsc.org

MIX
Paper from
responsible sources
FSC® C104740

Franklin Watts

An imprint of

Hachette Children's Group

Part of The Watts Publishing Group

Carmelite House

50 Victoria Embankment

London EC4Y 0DZ

An Hachette UK Company

www.hachette.co.uk

www.franklinwatts.co.uk

THIS DROP OF WATER

A LOOK AT THE WATER CYCLE

Anna Claybourne

Illustrated by
Sally Garland

W
FRANKLIN WATTS
LONDON • SYDNEY

CONTENTS

THUNDERSTORM!

It's a sunny, sweltering, boiling hot summer day. Everyone's in the garden. When suddenly ...

BOOM! A thunderstorm!

Here comes the rain!
Drops of water are falling from the sky.

Hundreds of them ...
thousands of them ...
millions of them!

Maybe we won't go for that picnic after all.
Oh no – our chalk pictures!
But I love the cool, refreshing rain.
I try to catch it on my tongue.

A drop of water falls and falls,
zooming down from the sky,
faster and faster. Until …
SPLAT! It hits me.
Right on the nose.

The **raindrops** soak into the hot, dusty ground.
They bounce and splat on the stones.
They patter on the leaves, and rattle on the roof.
I'm dripping wet!

But why do thunderstorms happen in summer?
Where does a drop of water come from, anyway?
And where does it go? **I want to know!**

WATERY WORLD

One drop of water, like this, is a teeny, tiny part of all the water in the world.

Our planet, the Earth, is **really watery**.
Huge seas and oceans cover more than half of it.
On the land, there's even more water
– like streams, rivers, lakes, ponds and puddles.

Altogether, that's a **lot** of drops of water.
How many? About 25 septillion drops!
That's a ginormous number that looks like this ...

25,000,000,000,000,000,000,000,000

THE EARTH

Sea

Land

Mercury

Venus

Earth

Mars

Jupiter

The Earth is the wettest planet.
It's mainly blue and white,
like a **swirly marble**,
thanks to all its water and the clouds all over it.
It looks like a **drop of water**
floating in space.

When we look far, far away into space,
we can see other planets.
They are not watery, like our world.
They are much drier.

The Earth's watery wonders

Longest river: River Nile, Africa – about 6,853 m long
Deepest lake: Lake Baikal, Russia – about 1,632 m deep
Biggest ocean: Pacific Ocean – about 165 million square km

9

IT CAME FROM OUTER SPACE

Where did all the water come from?
Nobody really knows.

Some say it came from
icy comets and asteroids,
crashing into the Earth.

Some say the rocks
that made the Earth
had water in them
from the start.

Maybe it's both.

At first, the Earth was very hot.
When the oceans first formed,
they were hot too, like a bath.

Nearly four billion years ago, life on Earth began.

Trilobite

Anomalocaris

Hallucigenia

The earliest animals were strange-looking water creatures.

11

FLOWING DOWNHILL

If I take a bucket of water and pour it out, what happens?

Most of the water in our world is liquid.
Liquids are runny. They flow and spill.
They form into drops that plop and splash.

If a liquid is on a slope,
the Earth's gravity pulls it down.

That's what happens when the rain falls, too.
Wherever it lands, the water heads **downhill** – until it can't go down any further.
Rain runs down from the **mountains** in fast-flowing streams.

Streams flow down into bigger, broader rivers.
Water tumbles down over waterfalls.
It collects in lakes and ponds.

Eventually rivers flow downwards into the **seas** and **oceans**, and fill them up.

13

INTO THE OCEANS

Why are the seas and oceans full of water?

Because they are the lowest parts of the Earth. They are where all the water collects.

As rivers flow to the sea, they wash salty minerals out of the rocks. That's why the sea is **so salty**.

Land is higher

Seabed is lower

The tides also make the sea flow UP and down the beach.

The seas and oceans are
ENORMOUS.
They stretch much, much further
than you can see.

Wind blows across the sea,
and pushes up waves.
The waves get bigger and bigger.
When they reach the beach,
the waves curl over and break.

The Moon and the Earth spin
around each other in space.
Every day, the Moon's gravity
pulls on the sea.
This creates the tides,
which make the sea rise and fall.

Surfers ride the waves as they move.

15

UNDERWATER

... there's a whole different world.

The animals here breathe in water, instead of air.

Animals need to breathe in a gas called **oxygen**. Mammals like us get our oxygen from the air, using our lungs.

But fish, and many other sea creatures, have gills. The water flows past the gills and they soak up oxygen from the water.

Breathe in ...

If we want to explore underwater, we have to wear special **diving gear**.

Whales are mammals too. They come to the surface to breathe air.

Submarines have air inside, for the crew to breathe.

OUT OF THE SEA

All day and all night, rivers flow into the sea. So why don't the seas get bigger?

As well as flowing into the sea,
water leaves the sea.
How does it get out? It evaporates.
That means the liquid water turns into a gas,
and floats away into the air.

Water
vapour

Liquid

The sun shines on the surface
of the sea, warming it up.
Water on the surface turns into gas,
called water vapour.

A gas can float around freely.
It doesn't flow downhill,
like liquid water.

The water vapour rises upwards,
into the sky.

Water evaporates into the air all the time.
It happens in other places too.

When we dry our washing in the garden,
the water in it turns into water vapour.
It floats off into the air.
The washing's dry!

The hot sun makes a puddle
evaporate and disappear.

Water evaporates from **lakes**,
rivers and **ponds** as well.

CLOUDY SKIES

At first you can't see the water vapour, or gas, going into the sky.

Water vapour is invisible.

But as it rises high up into the sky, it gets colder.
The cold makes the water start to condense,
or turn back into a liquid.
It clumps together in droplets – tiny drops of water.

The drops are so small that they can still float in the sky.
They reflect the sunlight, and this makes them look white.
We see them as white, fluffy clouds.
Each cloud is made up of millions of tiny drops!

Cirrus – high, wispy clouds

Cumulonimbus – a storm is on the way

The wind blows, making the clouds move.
Some **blow** around the **seas and oceans**.
Some blow over the land.
Look – they're coming this way!

Cumulus – seen in sunny weather

Clouds come in different shapes and patterns.
They all have their own names.
Can you spot all these in the sky?

Stratus – low, grey clouds that lead to fog and drizzle

HERE COMES THE RAIN!

When is a cloud ready to make rain?
When it gets cold enough.

As clouds rise higher into the sky,
they get colder.
If they blow into cool weather,
they get colder too.

In a cold cloud,
the water droplets stick together.
They make bigger, heavier raindrops.
The bigger drops block out light from the sun.
The cloud looks dark grey and gloomy.
It's a raincloud!

Soon, the drops are too big to float in the air.
They start to fall as raindrops.

Here comes the rain!

Now the water has come back to where it started ...

It fell from the sky ...
ran into streams and rivers ...
and flowed into the sea.

It turned into water vapour,
and rose into the air ...
made clouds ...
which blew over the land ...
and turned into rain again.

All the time,
water goes round and round.
It's called the **water cycle**.

23

THE BIG FREEZE

When it's really, *really* cold, water changes again. It turns into solid ice.

A liquid can **splash** and flow, but a **solid** is hard, and stays in one shape.

Snow is made of rain frozen into **ice crystals**.
Hail is rain frozen into hard, solid ice balls.
Icicles grow when **dripping** water freezes.

It's **freezing cold** on high mountains,
and at the icy South Pole.
They are covered in snow and ice.

In some countries, it's so cold that
ponds can **freeze** completely solid.
Sometimes people go skating on them.

(But it's best to keep away from frozen ponds, just in case!)

WATER SHAPES THE WORLD

As water flows, it feels soft and gentle. It drips and splashes in my hands.

But **flowing**, splashing water can be strong and powerful. It carves the land into valleys, cliffs, sand and pebbles. It makes our world the shape it is. A river slowly wears away the rock it flows across. Over a long time, it carves deep valleys.

Rocks **rolling** and **tumbling** in rivers become smooth pebbles. The pebbles **crash** against the river bed, and wear it away even more.

Waves **crash** onto the coast,
wearing away rocks.
They **crumble** and **fall**, making
cliffs, pebbles and sand.

A waterfall **hollows** out
a deep plunge pool
where it lands.

Rain and ice on mountains
wear down rock.
It **cracks**, crumbles
and **tumbles** downhill.

WATER UNDERGROUND

Not all the water flows into rivers and into the sea.

Some sinks down, down, down into the ground.

It soaks into the soil,
where plant roots can reach it.

Deeper underground,
there are rocks that can soak up water,
like a sponge.
Water soaks into the rocks, and gets held there.
It's called groundwater.

Wells collect groundwater.

Under the ground, some types of rock **dissolve** in water.
The water makes holes in the rock.
They get **bigger** and **bigger**, forming underground **caves** and **tunnels**.

Drip ...
drip ...
drip

Water drips from the roof.
Each drop leaves a bit of dissolved rock behind.
It makes a **stalactite!**
It's like a rock icicle.

The rock builds up on the floor too.
This is a **stalagmite!**

WATER FOR PLANTS

Plants make their own food using water, gas from the air and energy from sunlight.

To get water, plants suck it up through their roots. The water moves up the plant through tubes inside it. It spreads to all the parts of the plant.

Plants use this water,
and the energy from sunlight, to make food.
This is called **photosynthesis**.
When photosynthesis happens,
plants release water vapour from their leaves.

In fact, all living things need water to survive.
Living things are made of tiny cells.
For cells to work, they have to be filled with water.

WATER FOR ANIMALS

Animals need water too. They get water by drinking it.

Elephants love water. They suck it up into their trunks, then give themselves a shower!

Giraffes have to reach the water like this!

My **cat** hates water. But some big cats are good swimmers. This **lion** can swim. **Tigers** can too!

Crocodiles and **hippos** are river animals. They live mostly in the water.

What do animals do if there's no water?

Camels have humps that store fat. Their bodies use the fat to make extra water.

This **desert beetle** lets dew from the air collect on its body. Then it lifts up its tail, and the dew runs down into its mouth.

WATER FOR US

What happens when I drink a drop of water?

Water doesn't taste of much. It's easy to swallow.
Mmmmm, nice and cold.
The water goes down my throat,
and into my stomach.

From there, it goes into **my blood**,
and **all** around my body.

All your body parts need water ...
Organs like your brain and heart.
Body bits like muscles, bones and skin.
And all the tiny cells that build your body.

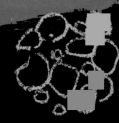

We need water to make sweat …
tears … and saliva (the spit in your mouth).
Spare water comes out as wee!
A bit of water comes out in your breath, too.
On a cold day, the tiny water droplets
make a mini cloud.

Every day, I have to drink about this much
water to stay healthy -----

But some of it comes from food, like a watery cucumber.

In fact, about two-thirds of me is made of water!
A baby is almost all water.
An old person, like a great-grandpa,
is just over half water.

TURN ON THE TAP!

I got this water from the tap. Just turn it on, and out comes the fresh clean water. Simple!

But hang on!

How did it get into the tap?

The water in the tap is part of the **water cycle**.

It mostly comes from the sky, as rain or snow.
It flows into streams and rivers.
We use big lakes called **reservoirs** to collect it.
We **pipe** the water to a water treatment plant.
(That's not a green, growing plant.
It's a place where water gets cleaned.)

Machines filter out leaves, twigs and **dirt**.
They add chemicals too, to kill germs.
The clean water flows into big mains water pipes ...
The mains pipes carry it to cities, towns and houses.
Inside the house, plumbing pipes take the water
to the taps, bath, shower and toilet.

DOWN THE PLUGHOLE

After a bath, or doing the washing up, the water flows away – down the plughole.

Where does it go?

Plumbing pipes take the water to the drains.

It flows down into big underground tunnels, called sewers.

The sinks, baths and toilets all lead to the sewer.

It's not just dirty water in here.

There's wee, poo, bits of old food …

It's **VERY** smelly.

Rats and cockroaches live here too.

sewer

water treatment plant

In a **big city**,
the clean water can go back
into the water pipes,
to be used again ... and again!

The sewer carries the dirty water to another
water treatment plant.
Here the water is cleaned in different ways.
Then it can flow back into rivers or the sea.

PRECIOUS WATER

We need water to stay alive.
And we need it to be clean.

If it's not, there could be germs and bugs in it,
and they can give you horrible diseases.

It takes a lot of work to clean water
and send it through pipes to my house.
That's why we shouldn't waste it.

I turn the tap off when I'm cleaning my teeth.
We don't spend an hour in the shower!

40

Some places don't have water treatment plants.

People drink water from wells, or straight from rivers
or ponds that can be dirty.

Some places have **droughts.**
That means there's not enough rain, and not enough water to drink.

A **flood** can be a disaster too. Muddy, dirty water swamps
homes and streets. It flows into the clean water supply,
and makes the water unsafe to drink.

Rescuers bring clean water to help people survive.
When people can get fresh, clean drinking water,
their lives are safer and happier.

Every drop is precious.

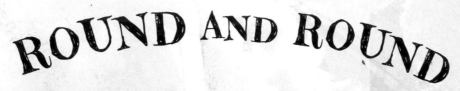

ROUND AND ROUND

**The thunderstorm has stopped,
the sun is shining, and now there's a rainbow!**

The sunlight **shines** into water droplets in the sky.
Inside each drop, the light bounces around,
and gets reflected back out.
This makes the white light break up into **rainbow colours**.
The storm is over, but there's more weather on the way.
The sky is still full of tiny water droplets.

There will be more **rain** ...
More **lakes** filling up ...
More **baths, showers** and **toilet** flushes ...
More water flowing in **rivers to the sea** ...
More **clouds** forming ...
And more rain falling again.

The water doesn't get old or get used up.
It just goes round and round and round,
in the water cycle.

WEIRD WATER

It's **all around us**, and inside us.
It's on the ground,
under the ground,
and in the sky.
We **drink it**, wash in it,
play and swim in it.

But water is also **VERY** strange.
When water freezes,
it gets **bigger** and lighter.
That's why ice floats.
Most liquids don't do that!

Even weirder, hot water
freezes faster than cold water.

44

The tiny molecules that water is made of **pull towards each other.**
They make a force called surface tension.
This is what makes a drop of water **hold** together.

It also gives water a 'skin'.
There's no skin really.
But the surface of water
acts as if it has one.
Small, light animals,
like water skaters,
can stand on top of it.

To a tiny insect, water feels very thick and sticky.

WATER ACTIVITIES

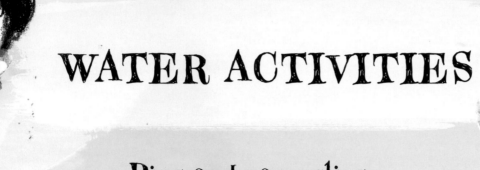

Pins and paperclips

Metal pins, needles and paperclips
are heavier than water.
If you drop them into a bowl of water,
they won't float. They will sink to the bottom.

But you can make them sit on top of the water,
because of **surface tension**.
Fill a bowl with water and let it get very still.
Now gently lie a metal paperclip on the surface.
If it's tricky, try using a piece of kitchen roll to lower it on.

Water cycle in a jar

Put some warm tap water in the bottom of a glass jar.
Put a small plate, or the upside-down jar lid,
over the top of the jar, with some ice cubes on top.

The water will start to **evaporate**, rise upwards and make clouds.
When it touches the cold plate or lid, it will **condense** into drops,
and rain back down.

Glass of water rainbow

Stand a glass of water on a piece of white paper, next to a sunny window.

As the sun shines into the glass of water, it will act like a water drop and split the sunlight into **rainbow** colours. You should be able to see them on the paper.

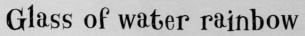

Growing ice

Fill a small plastic drinks bottle with water. Leave the lid off, and stand the bottle in the freezer (with some space above it).

Leave it overnight to freeze, then take it out. The water has grown, making a mini **ice tower!**

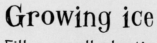

GLOSSARY

asteroid A lump of rock that orbits the sun.

cells The tiny units that living things are made from.

comet A ball of rock and ice that orbits the sun.

condense To change from a gas into a liquid.

drought A long time without rain.

flood When water flows over what is usually dry land.

evaporate To change from a liquid into a gas.

gas A light, usually invisible, spread-out state that water and other substances can exist in.

gills Organs found in fish and some other water animals, used to breathe underwater.

gravity A force that pulls things towards the middle of the Earth.

groundwater Water that collects underground.

liquid A runny, flowing state that water and other substances can exist in.

mammal A type of animal that feeds its babies on milk, such as humans, dogs, mice and whales.

minerals Natural, non-living substances found in the Earth, such as metals and gemstones.

molecules Tiny units that water and other substances are made from.

oxygen A gas found in air and water which animals need to breathe in to survive.

photosynthesis The way plants use energy from sunlight to make food and grow.

reservoir A lake (sometimes made by humans) used as storage for a water supply.

solid A firm state that keeps its shape, which water and other substances can exist in.

stalactite A long shape that forms inside caves and hangs down.

stalagmite A long structure that builds up from the floor of a cave.

surface tension A force that makes water cling together in drops, and makes it seem to have a 'skin'.

tides The regular rising and falling of sea levels about twice a day.

water cycle The way water moves from seas and oceans into the air, falls as rain, flows into rivers, and returns to the sea.

water vapour Water in the form of a gas.

INDEX

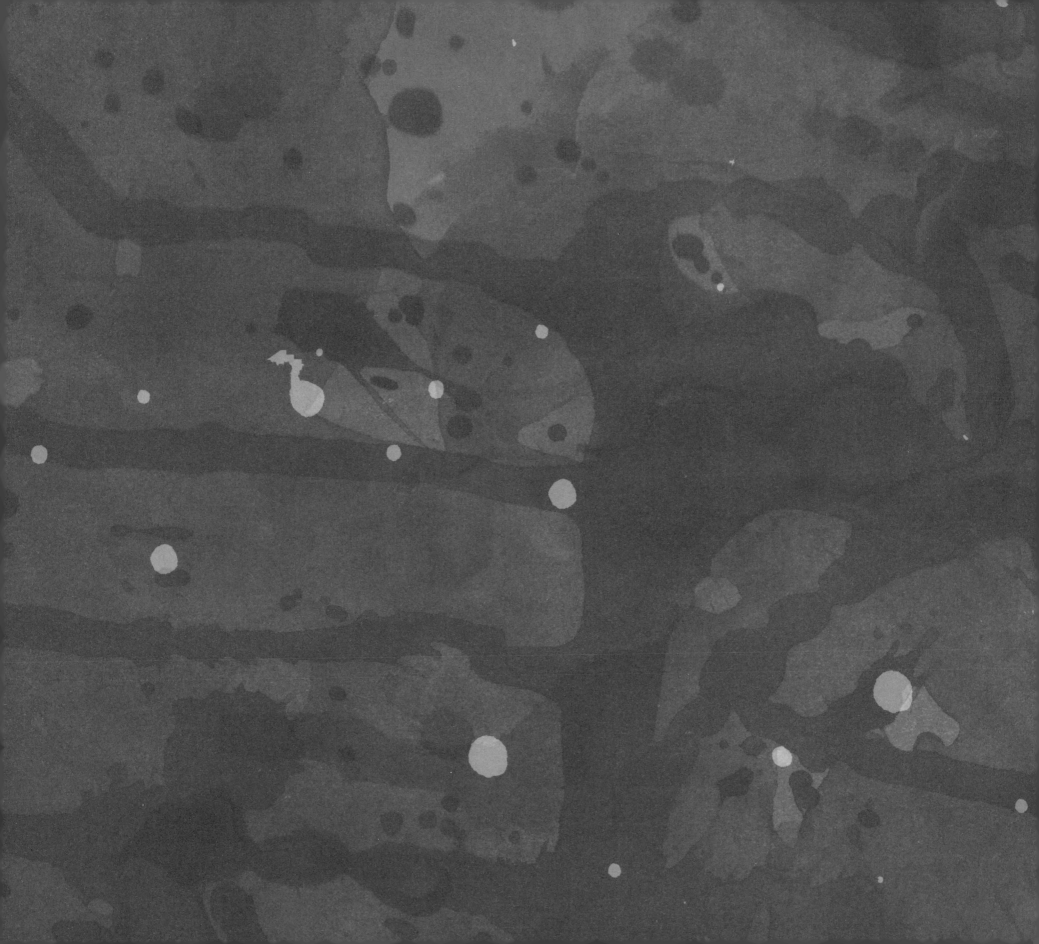

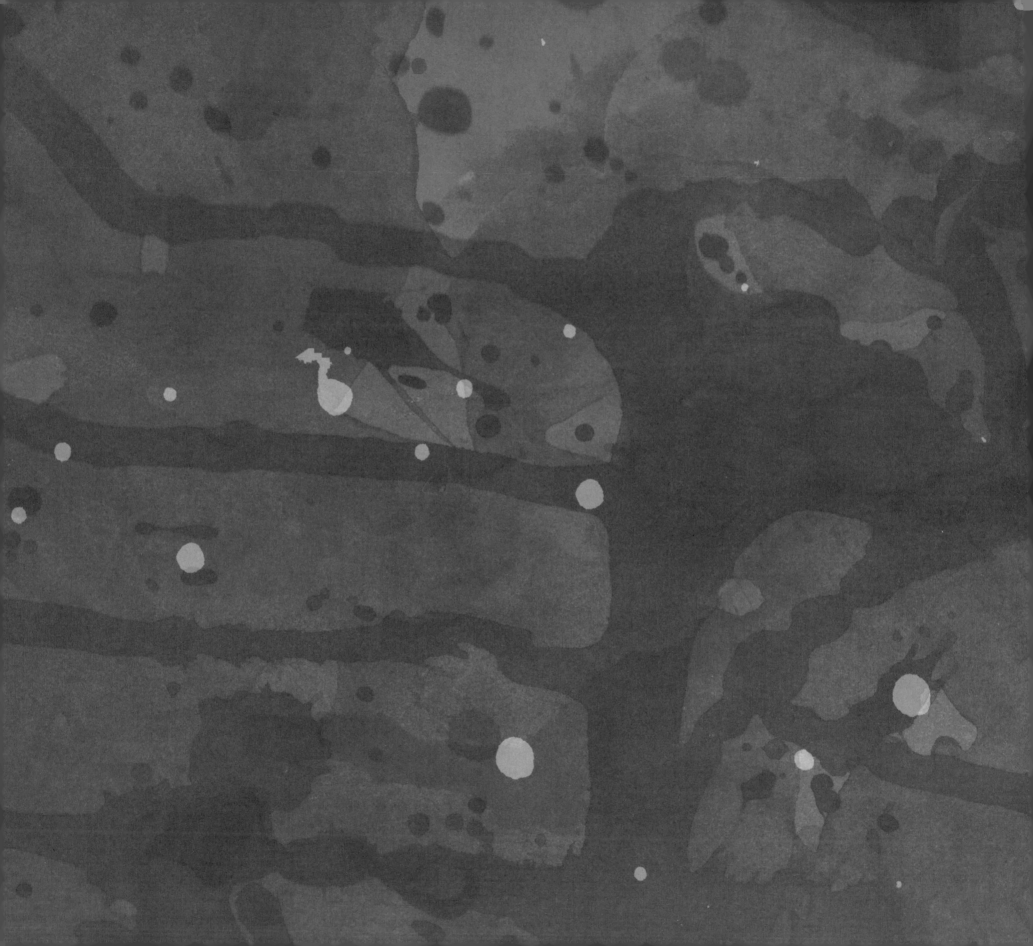